# Noah's Flood
## Local or
## Worldwide?

## Sylvia Penny

ISBN: 978-1-78364-491-9

## www.obt.org.uk

First edition 2003
Second edition 2018

**********

The Open Bible Trust
Fordland Mount, Upper Basildon,
Reading, RG8 8LU, UK.

# Noah's Flood
## Local or Worldwide?

## Contents

# Introduction

# Introduction

Just as there are different views amongst Christians over the subject of *Creation*, so are there over the subject of *Noah's Flood*. Creation is described in just two short chapters of the Bible, Genesis 1 and 2, and Noah's flood is described in four chapters, Genesis chapters 6 to 9.

There are some people who dismiss Noah's flood and consider that it never took place. It is either irrelevant to them, or they go along with the secular explanation that the Biblical story was copied from the Babylonian flood traditions. The Flood narrative is found in Tablet 11 of the Gilgamesh Epic, which was recorded on twelve Akkadian tablets, dated about 2000-1700 B.C., and it is this record which some consider to be the source of the Biblical story.

However, most Christians, especially those who believe that the Bible is the inspired word of God, take the description of Noah's flood literally. Among these, there are different literal interpretations of the flood, which fall into two main categories:

     (1)  Noah's flood was worldwide
     (2)  Noah's flood was a local flood.

We shall be looking at the pros and cons of these two opposing points of view later in this booklet. However, first perhaps we should ask if it *matters* whether there was a flood or not.

## Does it matter whether there was a flood?

In answer to this question, if the Bible has recorded that there was a flood, but we do not believe that the flood ever took place, we have to question whether we really accept the fact that the Bible is the inspired Word of God. Our personal worldview will affect what we believe to be the truth about Noah's flood. If we do **not** believe in the inspiration of Scripture, then it is unlikely that we will believe that Noah's flood took place at all, and will dismiss it as being a myth, an ancient legend or story blown vastly out of all proportion to reality. No worldly-wise person today would believe God covered the whole world with water, or even a large part of it, centred somewhere in the Middle East! However, there is much we still do not know about our world and our universe, especially about what actually happened in the distant past. What we do know pales into insignificance against what we don't know. Therefore, if God tells us in the Bible that something is a fact, the Christian is wise to accept this, rather than to go along with man's wisdom.

For me then, as a Christian who believes the Bible, it is not an option to believe that there was no flood. If I believe that the Bible is God-breathed, then I believe all that it contains, even if it is difficult to understand *how* it can be. I am always mindful of Mary's words to Gabriel after being informed that she was to be the mother of Jesus, the Christ – "How will this be, since I am a virgin?" (Luke 1:34). Her question was asked, not in disbelief, but in not understanding *how* this could possibly be accomplished. Similarly with the flood. It is a matter of not understanding *how* God did it, not of querying *whether* He did it.

However, it is not only the inspiration of Scripture that leads me to accept that the flood was a historical fact. It is also the Lord's own reference to it as a fact in the Gospels.

> "Just as it was in the days of Noah, so also will it be in the days of the Son of Man. People were eating, drinking, and marrying and being given in marriage up to the day Noah

entered the ark. Then the flood came and destroyed them all." (Luke 17:26,27).

Thus, if the inspiration of Scripture is important to us, and if what the Lord stated to be a *fact* while He was on earth is important to us, then the fact that a flood took place must also be important to us.

Having established that it *does* matter that there was a flood, we then have to ask if it matters whether it was worldwide or just a local flood. Both of these opposing points of view are held by Christians who uphold Scripture as the inspired word of God. It is their *interpretations* of the chapters describing the flood that differ. To me, therefore, it is not quite so important whether we accept that the flood was worldwide, or whether we think it was local. As we shall see, both points of view have some good arguments in their favour.

# 1:
# Who holds
# which view?

# 1: Who holds which view?

Even as Christians who believe in the inspiration of Scripture, our personal worldview will still affect what we believe to be the truth about Noah's flood. Although we believe the flood took place, there are broadly speaking two different ways in which we can understand this fact. One is that God sent a worldwide flood, and the other is that it was a large, yet restricted flood, covering a large area of land somewhere in the Middle East. Generally speaking, our beliefs about how and when God created the world affect the way we understand Noah's flood.

## Worldwide flood

Those who believe God created the world only six to ten thousand years ago *tend* to believe that Noah's flood was worldwide. They reject all modern theories of geology and explanations of how the geological layers were formed, their dating, and what the fossils in them mean. They have replaced this with a system of 'flood geology' whereby the worldwide flood supplies an explanation for many of the unusual geological formations we see today. There are differences of opinion among these *Young-Earth Creationists* as to the *mechanics* of the flood, but they are all agreed that it was worldwide, and that its results can be seen in the rock formations we are left with today. Henry Morris, the president of the Institute for Creation Research, co-authored a book entitled *The Genesis Flood* with John Whitcomb, which was first produced in 1961. However, when he wrote the book, Morris was the Professor and Head of the Department of Civil Engineering at Virginia Polytechnic Institute. This gives an excellent and detailed apologetic for Young-Earth Creationism and for the universality of the flood. It provides a wealth of information and documented sources of all the various views and beliefs held on the flood over the centuries, together with their reasons for not subscribing to the *local flood theory*.

However, they are not the only group of Christians who subscribe to a worldwide flood. There are those who may not be *Young-Earth Creationists*, but who still hold to the worldwide flood of Noah. Of these, Dr. Victor Pearce is one, and he has written a series of books under the general title "Evidence for Truth". The first, which is on the subject of Science (written in 1998), includes a section explaining his personal view of how the flood of Noah was worldwide, but he rejects the idea that this was responsible for all the geological rock formations we have today. He agrees with most scientists today that the world itself was created over billions of years.

## Local flood

The local flood theory tends to be upheld by those who believe the world is billions of years old, rather than just a few thousand, although there are exceptions to this, as mentioned above.

Arthur Custance, who is a contender for the *Gap Theory* of creation (see the Open Bible Trust booklet, *Theories of Creation*, by the author), has written various papers supporting the local flood view, including Doorway Publications *The Flood: Local or Global?* and *Flood Traditions of the World*. His argument for a local flood includes the proviso that although it was only local in extent, it was universal *so far as mankind was concerned*. In other words, at the time of the flood, people all lived in one area of the world, so that the flood wiped all human beings out, but left most other things intact.

Hugh Ross, who favours the *Day-Age Theory* of creation, also supports the local flood theory, and similarly considers that all human beings were wiped out at the time. He has produced various tapes and literature explaining and supporting this view from Scripture.

Bernard Ramm put forward a more unusual opinion on the flood. (His views on creation are similar to the *Day-Age Theory.*) In 1954 he wrote what was a fairly influential book at the time, entitled *The Christian View of Science and Scripture*. In this he stated his opinion that not only was Noah's flood local in extent, but that it only wiped out *some* human beings, those with whom God was angry at the time. When Whitcomb and Morris subsequently produced their book *The Genesis Flood,* a whole chapter was devoted to refuting this particular view.

In this book, unless otherwise stated, all quotations from the authors mentioned above come from the books listed in the bibliography at the back of this book.

## Which view do we hold?

It can be seen then, that how some people view Noah's flood depends upon how they view creation. One tends to follow from the other. Conversely, those who have no fixed ideas on how and when God created, are unlikely to have any fixed views on how and when God flooded the earth. We may accept both at face value and leave it at that. However, for some Christians this is unsatisfactory, and so it is necessary to look at the details of both views.

# 2:
# When was the flood?

# 2: When was the flood?

Apart from Arthur Custance, all those mentioned above date the flood as occurring some time before 4000 B.C. Custance states that Biblical chronology does not allow for the flood being much earlier than 5000 years ago, which gives a date of around 3000 B.C. However, he recognises that accepting such a late date for the reduction of the world's population to only eight people goes against all the current anthropological and archaeological evidence to the contrary.

Henry Morris states that "Near Eastern cultures apparently have a rather continuous archaeological record back to at least the fifth millennium B.C." which means that the flood would have to have occurred before this date. Morris therefore goes on to argue that the pre-Abrahamic chronology can be extended by careful examination of Genesis, and concludes that the flood could have occurred at any time between three and five thousand years *before* Abraham's birth, which he dates at 2,167 B.C. This certainly gives more room for manoeuvre.

Hugh Ross is generally more vague over the dating, and suggests a flood date of anywhere between 6,000 and 12,000 B.C., again designed to coincide more with scientific thinking about when modern man arose, and at what dates he began to spread over the earth.

Bernard Ramm states that the early Babylonian and Egyptian civilizations are dated earlier than 4,000 B.C., and that the end of the ice-age was about 10,000 B.C. He therefore believes the flood occurred before 4,000 B.C., but after 10,000 B.C.

Some scientists think that the Indians arrived in America, and the Aborigines spread to Australia up to 12,000 years ago, just after the ice-age. However, this is rather difficult to fit in with any flood scenario. What seems certain is that the further back in time we go, the more vague becomes the dating, *both* by scientists, and by theologians!

Victor Pearce, who has a particular interest in anthropology and prehistoric archaeology, however, presents some interesting facts in his book *Evidence for Truth: Science*, about the possible dating of the flood, which he places between 4,000 and 5,000 B.C. He refers to a worldwide disappearance of life around 5,000 B.C. that he supports with a number of scientific facts. He asserts:

> Scientists have been at a loss to account for the disappearance of culture and life in the Old World between the Copper Stone Age and the Bronze Age. If they accepted the Flood as an explanation, it would solve their enigma. Some have described this in various terms. It has been called 'the hiatus', 'the gap', 'the sterile period' and 'the yawning millennium'. This hiatus, as we call it, occurs in Egypt, around the Mediterranean and in the Middle East and India and probably in China. The inhabitants of Europe were also wiped out by the Flood. It was one thousand years before new people repopulated it, by the new migration from Ararat. They are called by archaeologists, the second Danubians, because they migrated along the River Danube, as had the first Danubians before the flood.

He also refers to the same gap existing in the New World, and quotes from Dr. Stephen Bedwell's *Oregon University Notes* (1975) which state:

> "Examination of all these areas reveals a hiatus of 1,300 years between 5100 B.C. and 3000 B.C. in the radio-active record, a hiatus which is real."

The areas referred to are all in the USA, and there are a number of reports by different American scientists working in different universities who have all commented upon the same existing gap. However, none have attributed the existence of this gap to a worldwide flood! Varying alternative suggestions have always been made. Significantly, however, *before* this gap the bones of the modern type of horse, and other animals such as elephants, camels, lions and tigers have been found. *After* the gap, none have been found. The Spaniards re-introduced the horse to America in the seventeenth century, and terrified the natives living there, who had never seen a horse before! Combined with this evidence of a gap in civilisation, culture, and the existence of certain types of animals in particular areas, there is also evidence of a change of climate and environment right across North America.

This climate change has also been documented in the Egyptian civilisation where, before the gap, Egypt's valleys were wet marshlands, the land was well wooded, and what is now the Sahara desert was very fertile with lush green growth. Cave drawings in the Sahara depicted game animals, whereas after the gap these disappeared. The land became barren and dry. Also, fossil tropical plants have been found in present-day Polar Regions, and these have been dated at before 4000 B.C. Many discoveries such as these have been made by scientists over the years. These are *not* in dispute. However, it is the different theories that explain these facts that are disputed. Each discovery is like another piece in a large jigsaw puzzle for which no picture has been supplied, and for which, it still seems, the majority of the pieces are still missing! Many of those who believe in the inspiration of Scripture often try to link the facts relating to climate and environment change in the past to Noah's flood. The scientific explanations of these Christians vary, but they all desire to prove Noah's flood took place. Also, as we can see, it is difficult to date the flood, which is why most commentators do not attempt to do so with any degree of precision.

# 3:
# What caused
# the flood?

# 3: What caused the flood?

Many books and booklets on the subject of the flood include detailed explanations of how the flood probably occurred, what caused it, where all the water came from, and where it all went afterwards. I do not intend to go into many details here, but just to provide an overview of some of the ideas that have been suggested by different Christians over the years. To be fair, most of these people have made it clear that their ideas are still only theories, and not the final answer, as none of these views has ever been proven beyond doubt, and may never be so, as it is impossible to recreate what happened in the past, and so test the theory.

## Local flood theories

Those who believe in a local flood have an easier job than those who believe in a worldwide flood, as the generally accepted scientific position is that there is no evidence for a worldwide flood. However, Bernard Ramm, who believed that the flood was local, is the first to admit that:

> "the weight of evidence for the local flood is actually showing the imponderable difficulties of a universal flood."

In other words, his starting point was that belief in a worldwide flood was scientifically untenable, and therefore it must have been local. He stated:

"A local flood could come and go and leave no trace after a few thousand years, but could a universal flood be a traceless flood?"

His main point, therefore, was that as there is no distinctive geological proof of a universal flood, it must have been local.

He also discussed the problem of the amount of water required by a universal flood. If all the water *in the air* fell at the same time, it would only be seven inches deep. To cover the highest mountains would require eight times more water than now exists in the whole world including that in the oceans. In order to cover the Himalayas, the water would have to be six miles deep. Flood deposits found in Mesopotamia consist of various strata of clay, one at Warka (Erech), one at Kish (1.5 feet), one at Ur (8 feet), and one at Shuruppak. To a certain extent, these deposits show that a local flood *cannot* come and go without a trace, but they also show that if water six miles deep all over the earth had ever existed, presumably there should be some sort of geological evidence to show for it. With such arguments as these, Bernard Ramm dispensed with the worldwide flood theory.

In its place he believed that a local flood was produced by a combination of rain, and ocean movement in the Mesopotamian valley. He also thought some special geological phenomenon occurred as indicated by the Biblical expression "on that day all the springs of the great deep burst forth", (Genesis 7:11). This, he considered, caused the ocean waters to creep up the Mesopotamian valley. The ark would have been carried up to somewhere in the Ararat range of mountains, and then a reversal of the geological phenomenon resulted in the water draining back into the ocean from the valley. He concludes that as it was a local flood of short duration there would not be any specific evidence of it left after over six thousand years of weathering.

Hugh Ross expresses similar views, but considers that the water did not drain back into the ocean, but instead evaporated over nine months. He states that the Mesopotamian valley is the only place in the world that has geological evidence of a flood over a large area at the right time in history to coincide with the Genesis flood. Other areas show evidence of widespread flooding, but are dated at the wrong time to be equated with Noah's flood.

Arthur Custance, although also believing in the local flood theory, places this in the Iranian Highland Plateau, around Armenia. He points out that on the Black Sea there is a raised beach 750 feet up the mountain, and that although the Caspian Sea, the Sea of Aral and Lake Balkash have no outlets (and thus should be salty like the Dead Sea), their waters are still comparatively fresh, and that therefore they must be of recent origin. He therefore suggests this could be the result of flooding in the area, and considers this to be Noah's flood.

However, apart from Bernard Ramm, most who hold to the local flood theory believe it wiped out all mankind, apart from the eight people in the ark. This presents a different problem in that it is generally accepted that humans had spread beyond the 'cradle of civilisation' in Mesopotamia long before the time of Noah's flood. Yet in order to hold this view, it is necessary to believe that all humans were still living within this very small area of the earth's surface. Thus in solving (part of) the geological problem by supposing Noah's flood was local, an anthropological problem is created.

In addition, although it is easier to imagine a local flood taking place, it has been pointed out that even this poses a number of geological difficulties. Firstly, non-Christian scientists do not accept that such a large flood ever took place in the Middle East at the required time in history, mainly because there is no evidence for one! The flood deposits mentioned earlier at Kish, Ur, and so on, have been proven to cover just a fraction of the area required by the local flood theory.

Also, the scenario described by Bernard Ramm is based upon a hypothesis put forward by a 19th century writer, Hugh Miller, who suggested that the local flood resulted from the Near East sinking at a rate of 400 feet a day, reaching a depth of 16,000 feet in 40 days, so that the ocean waters poured into a huge saucer thus created, and covered the mountains that were in it. This is the 'geological phenomenon' which Ramm refers to, but which he never gives details of, as there is no historical or geological evidence that such an event ever took place.

Also, as indicated above, a number of flood deposits found in Mesopotamia have been found and dated at different times in history. However, although some of these have left deposits of clay as thick as 8 feet, none of these indicate a local flood anywhere near as extensive as the one required by Genesis to wipe out the entire human population, and to cover an area of 100,000 square miles. The argument put forward by some is that if comparatively small floods leave 8 foot clay deposits, then *presumably* floods lasting over a year, and covering over 100,000 square miles should leave a correspondingly large amount of evidence afterwards, none of which has been found. It seems therefore, from the purely geological point of view, there are difficulties in demonstrating there was *any* sort of flood at all – whether local, or worldwide.

To be fair, however, maybe it is the predetermination of what constitutes evidence that creates the problem. After all, the raised beaches on the Black Sea mentioned above require an explanation, together with the freshness of the water in the Caspian Sea, the Aral Sea, and Lake Balkash. Again, it would seem that one's presuppositions as to what happened in the past colour one's interpretation of the facts, as well as *which* facts are significant and require explanation.

## Worldwide flood theories

Young-Earth Creationists who believe that Noah's flood was worldwide have their own detailed explanations as to where all the water came from, and where it all went to after the flood. Henry Morris, in *The Genesis Flood,* supported what is referred to as the canopy theory. Briefly, this supposes that before the flood the earth was surrounded by a great vapour canopy, but for more on this see the *Appendix*. It suggests that Genesis 1:6,7 referred to a vast bank of water above the sky:

> And God said, "Let there be an expanse between the waters to separate water from water." So God made the expanse and separated the water under the expanse from the water above it.

It was also believed that there was no rain until the flood, but that the earth was watered by streams which came up from the ground, as mentioned in Genesis 2:5,6:

> For the Lord God had not sent rain on the earth and there was no man to work the ground, but streams came up from the earth and watered the whole surface of the ground.

At Noah's flood, the entire vapour canopy collapsed and produced a global rain lasting forty days. Morris acknowledged that a global flood could not be produced by the water in our present atmosphere, as even if it all suddenly precipitated at the same time, it would only cover the ground to a depth of two inches, (although as we have seen Ramm stated this would have been seven inches)!

This fact also means that the water that produced the flood must still be on the earth, as it is obviously not in the atmosphere. He therefore asserts that oceans today are much larger than they were before the flood, and that land areas are smaller. There is *some* evidence in support of this, in that some sea-levels were once much lower relative to the land surfaces than at present. Also, there are a number of canyons now under the sea, which look as if they must have been formed before being submerged, as they are similar in every respect to river canyons formed on land.

Morris also says it was likely that there were great geological upheavals at the flood, forming deep ocean basins and troughs, elevating land masses and forming mountains not previously there. Thus the high mountains were formed during the flood and so less water was initially required to cover the earth. In addition, all the geological strata laid down, together with their fossils, are attributed to this one huge catastrophe. This theory of geology is referred to as 'flood geology', and is rejected by all scientists other than *Young-Earth Creationists. The Genesis Flood* gives detailed explanations of this theory, together with supporting evidence.

Although flood geology is generally accepted by Young-Earth Creationists, Morris' explanation of where all the water came from originally has been questioned, and has since been rejected on scientific grounds by some of them. For example, in his book, *In the Beginning* (published in 1980), Walt Brown, who is a very keen Young-Earth Creationist, has demonstrated how he believes that it would be impossible for such a canopy of water above the earth to have existed. He puts forward the theory that the earth had a large volume of subterranean water contained in interconnected chambers that collectively formed a thin, spherical shell just over half a mile thick and about 10 miles below the earth's surface. There is some evidence for subterranean water, as in the world's deepest hole, drilled on the Kola Peninsula in northern Russia to a depth of seven and a half miles, hot flowing mineralised water was found, including salt water. The theory is that at Noah's flood, the earth's crust ruptured along the mid-oceanic ridge (a 46,000 mile long ridge which wraps around the earth, and most of which lies on the ocean floor), releasing most of the subterranean water and producing a vast, worldwide fountain of torrential rain, and muddy hail. Again, they claim this theory answers a number of scientific questions, including the intriguing question of how large numbers of woolly mammoths died, when they were living in what were temperate zones at the time. Evidence indicates they died instantaneously, and were preserved intact, and this, it is suggested, could have been the result of being suddenly encased in icy hail.

One particular advantage of accepting 'flood geology', as we saw above, is that the mountain ranges as we know them are believed to have been formed during the flood. Therefore it is not necessary to explain how there was enough water to cover the Himalayas, as they did not exist! Instead, it is believed that only low, undulating hills existed before, which means that far less water would be required to completely cover the earth's surface.

## Another worldwide flood theory

Dr Victor Pearce, although rejecting 'flood geology' and the Young-Earth theory, nevertheless holds to a worldwide flood theory. He provides many details of his view in his book *Evidence for Truth: Science,* which is based upon the belief that the world suffered a sudden change of axis, which was the cause of a worldwide flood. With this view, there is no problem explaining where the water came from, and where it went to, as the flood was merely a result of the redistribution of the existing water throughout the world, and the whole process took just over one year from start to finish. The idea that the tilting of the earth on its axis produced the flood was put forward as a suggestion many years ago. It was mentioned, and dismissed, by Bernard Ramm without any further comment in his book *The Christian View of Science and Scripture*. However, it is interesting to note that in several flood traditions throughout the world (notably in the Eskimos, Greenland, Mexico, Polynesia and India) the earth is referred to as tilting violently, shaking or turning over. These flood traditions are looked at more closely in chapter 8.

It has been scientifically proven that the outer crust of the earth now turns on a different axis to one previously, and that although such a change could happen, it would be expected to happen very slowly over long periods of time. However, it has also happened comparatively quickly at least once in the past. A quick change of axis would produce a worldwide flood, because the rotational speed and direction of the water on the earth's surface would have to suddenly readjust, and the water would initially flow turbulently and chaotically, before it settled in its new state of equilibrium.

The oceans are three times deeper than the earth's mountains, and cover nearly three times more of the world than the area of the continents, so that when they were displaced by an axis change they would have rushed over the mountains, sweeping everything in their path with them, including all animals and humans. Dr. Pearce also mentions the existence of even more water under the earth (as reported in the *New Scientist* in 1997), in addition to the oceans, which a change of axis could well have disrupted, causing that also to break out at the time of the flood. He cites a further edition of the *New Scientist* which reported that the waters of the Black Sea experienced a 'bursting out' about 5000 B.C., when apparently there was a sudden change from freshwater snails to seawater snails when the Black Sea was invaded by salt water.

Therefore, as a consequence of more up to date scientific research, it seems more likely that the water for Noah's flood was partially provided by water stored under the earth, rather than by a canopy of water above the earth. The present-day existence of such water has been proven by deep hole drilling, and has been reported in the secular scientific press by those with no religious views to substantiate.

To further support the idea of an axis change causing Noah's flood, Dr. Pearce points out the number of elevated fossil sea beaches throughout the world, some of which are just sixty feet above sea level, others hundreds and some even thousands of feet above sea level. On the other hand, there are many places that are now below sea level which once were dry land. It is a fact that sea levels have changed dramatically throughout the world – some are higher, some are lower. The only reasonable explanation for this, according to Dr. Pearce, would be an axis change that produced a redistribution of ocean and sea water throughout the world. As the earth rotates, the centrifugal force around the equator would be greatest and thus any water there would bulge and be at its deepest. If the axis changed, then the water level at the old equator would drop significantly and the water depth at the new equator would rise.

A further point to support this is that the old equator would have been at right angles to the magnetic pole, which means it would have passed through some of the highest mountain ranges in the world, including the Andes and the Himalayas. If this were the old equator, this would be expected, as the earth would have bulged due to the centrifugal force exerted, and produced higher mountains wherever the original equator happened to be.

He also includes many other details in support of this theory. In particular he describes many facts relating to the mysteries of an ancient city called Tiahuanaco in the Andes, and of Lake Titicaca. Although the city is now in icy latitudes of 12,000 feet above sea level, it was apparently built for a hot, tropical climate, it was a harbour city with docks and quays, and there is evidence that it was suddenly overwhelmed by a flood. There is also a fossil beach that runs for thousands of miles through the Andes, and Lake Titicaca is filled with salt sea water.

A change of axis, which produced Noah's flood, would explain all these mysteries and many other besides.

## Summary

After this brief look at a number of the geological theories of what caused the flood, where all the water came from, and where it all went afterwards, it can be seen that the number of facts available are both numerous and complicated. There are still many unexplained mysteries, geological and otherwise, and the same facts can be interpreted in different ways to prove different theories. All this being the case, it is almost an impossible puzzle to figure out for certain what actually happened thousands of years ago. That is why it is possible for Christians to hold different explanations, as each theory has quite a number of facts in its favour.

Therefore in the next three chapters we will turn to another approach, and will consider the details relating to the events before, during and after the flood, as recorded in the Bible. Maybe the interpretation of the Biblical narrative will clarify what happened at the flood more readily than the interpretation of the geological evidence available.

# 4:
# Before
# the flood
## (Genesis 6:5 – 7:10)

# 4: Before the flood (Genesis 6:5 – 7:10)

In these verses in Genesis we are given:

1) the reason for the flood,
2) the reason the ark was built, and
3) the reason the ark was filled with animals.

However, within these few verses we also find the reasons for the different views held by Christians on the flood. Most of these differences are caused by attempts to understand *how* God achieved what is described here, not *what* is described here. Again, the main differences in understanding fall into two groups, those who believe in a local flood and those who believe in a worldwide flood.

## 1) The reason for the flood

In Genesis 6:5,6 we read of God's judgement of man on earth in Noah's day:

> The Lord saw how great man's wickedness on the earth had become, and that every inclination of the thoughts of his heart was only evil all the time. The Lord was grieved that he had made man on the earth, and his heart was filled with pain.

Verse 11 adds that the earth was full of violence, and that all the people on earth had corrupted their ways. Noah was the only exception. He found favour in God's eyes, and was described as righteous and blameless among all the people living at that time. As a result, God decided to wipe mankind from the face of the earth, apart from Noah and his family, eight people altogether. He told Noah His intentions, and that He was going to destroy all the people on the earth with a flood in order to put an end to all the violence. Interestingly, once the flood was over, one of the few commands that God gave to Noah and his family was concerning shedding the blood of another human. Genesis 9:5-6 says:

> And from each man, too, I will demand an accounting for the life of his fellow man. "Whoever sheds the blood of man, by man shall his blood be shed; for in the image of God has God made man."

It seems that murder, as initiated by Cain when he attacked his brother Abel and killed him through jealousy (Genesis 4:8), had become the norm in the pre-flood society, and that the only way to eradicate this behaviour was for God to virtually begin all over again.

## World population at the time of the flood

We then come to the question of how many people God destroyed at the flood, to which of course there can be no straightforward answer. This depends on a number of factors including when we date the flood, and how many years we think elapsed between the creation of Adam and the flood. Suggestions have been made from around 4.5 billion people down to a few million at most. In other words, it is not really possible to know.

Those who believe in a local flood tend to stress reasons that there would be a low population (wars, murders, old age before first children born, and so on), as they have the entire world's population living in and around the Mesopotamian valley. They also mention that archaeological evidence indicates that the population cannot have been larger than a few million. Some have speculated that murder and violence were so normal that this in itself served to reduce the population dramatically.

Those who believe in a worldwide flood point out that people lived, on average, for hundreds of years before the flood. Thus they would each have had time to have large families. They therefore calculate that with a minimum of 1,656 years between Adam and the flood (using Biblical genealogies as a basis) there would be at least one billion people alive at the time of the flood, and very likely significantly more, especially if there are some gaps in the genealogies as many people have suggested. If this is correct, then it is unlikely that such a large population would have remained in one restricted area in the Middle East, and therefore this provides another argument in favour of a worldwide flood. In answer to the point that the archaeological evidence indicates that the population can only have been a few million, it is argued that a worldwide flood would have destroyed much of the evidence for a larger population.

Also, as mentioned previously, anthropological evidence suggests that the world's population had spread out beyond the Mesopotamian valley long before the date of the flood. In order to believe that the flood was local, and that it destroyed the entire human population, it is important that no human remains discovered elsewhere in the world are ever dated prior to the date of the flood. Unfortunately, this is not the case, so if we take this view it would be either necessary to question the standard dating techniques used by scientists, or we would have to date the flood earlier than the dates for any human remains found outside the Mesopotamian valley.

## Does 'all' mean 'all'?

As we have seen, apart from Bernard Ramm who was an exception to the rule, it is generally believed by both local flood and worldwide flood advocates, that the entire human population was drowned in the flood. Thus when such words as *all people* and *all mankind* are used in Genesis, both sides are in agreement. However, when such expressions as *all the earth* and *all life* and *every creature* and *all the high mountains* are used, differences of opinion emerge. Those who believe in a worldwide flood take these words at their face value and say they do mean 'all' in a universal sense, whereas those who believe in a local flood say they should be understood within a context. For example *all the earth* would mean *all the land,* and *all life* would mean only *life in that area*, and so on.

Arthur Custance shows that the Hebrew word which is translated *earth* in Genesis 6:4-6 has been translated, according to *Young's Analytical Concordance,* as

> "*country* 140 times, *ground* 96 times, and *earth* and *land* frequently (*earth* about 677 times and *land* 1,458 times). It is also rendered *field* once and by several other words in a very small number of instances."

Therefore, when the flood account refers to all the earth, it may actually mean all the land, or all the country, thus restricting it to one area on the earth.

Similarly it is considered that 'all the high mountains' refer only to those within this specific area. 'All life' refers only to life associated with the corrupting influence of man within this area, and that 'every creature' is similarly restricted in meaning.

As an example of this, if we read through the short book of Zephaniah we will see 1:2-3 refers to sweeping away everything from the face of the earth, including men, birds, fish and animals, and yet only a few verses later it is clearly referring to the land of Judah and the surrounding countries. The word translated "earth" is translated "land" in a number of translations, including the King James Version, and by doing so it clarifies the meaning of the passage.

In further support of the local flood theory, Psalm 104:5-9, which refers to the original creation and not the flood, says "*never again will the waters cover the earth*", which does seem to support the local flood theory.

However, Custance does suggest that Noah himself may have thought that God meant the entire world. In fact, he states that Noah "was assured that all mankind would be destroyed, and he probably supposed that the Flood would therefore be universal." Whether Custance is correct in this supposition is for us to decide.

## 2) The reason the ark was built

If we believe in a worldwide flood, then the reason for building an ark is pretty obvious – it was to save Noah and his family, and all the animals from drowning in the flood. In Genesis 6:17 God told Noah:

> "I am going to bring floodwaters on the earth to destroy all life under the heavens, every creature that has the breath of life in it. Everything on earth will perish."

In order to avoid sharing their fate, God gave Noah detailed instructions on how to build an ark in which he, his wife, his three sons and their wives were to be saved, along with every kind of animal, creature and bird.

However, if we believe in a local flood, then we have to explain why an ark was necessary. Why did Noah not simply migrate to safety, along with his family, leaving the rest of humanity to their fate? The main answer given by Arthur Custance, and others who believe in a local flood, is that the building of the ark was to serve as a warning to humanity of the impending judgement from God. He says:

> "It is doubtful whether God could have chosen a more effective way of making sure that while everyone was warned, no one who believed the message need be lost. But this is true only if the existing population of the earth was small enough in numbers or confined enough in settlement to hear about the undertaking."

He suggests that if the flood were to be worldwide, and the population had already spread over the earth, then there was no way that everyone would have seen or heard of their impending doom. Unfortunately for this view, however, there is nowhere in Scripture that tells us that the ark was to serve as a warning to humanity as a whole. Hebrews 11:7 is taken to support this view, which says:

> "By faith Noah, when warned about things not yet seen, in holy fear built an ark to save his family. By his faith he condemned the world and became heir of the righteousness that comes by faith."

The fact that his faith condemned the world is not the same as saying that everyone in the world saw, or heard about, the building of the ark, although it may have been that by the time it was complete, many *had* heard the story of an impending flood.

Another drawback to simply migrating would be that anybody who chose to do so could have followed Noah and his family to safety, so that not all the ungodly would have perished in the local flood. He could have migrated secretly, thus being the only one to escape, but then he would not have served as a warning to others, which Custance considers the main reason for the ark.

## How long did Noah take to build the ark?

The time taken for the building of the ark is usually mentioned by most people when considering the flood. Genesis 6:3 says:

> "Then the Lord said, "My Spirit will not contend with man for ever, for he is mortal; his days will be a hundred and twenty years.""

This is often taken to mean that at this point there were 120 years to go before the flood, and so Noah spent all of this time, or at least most of it, building the ark. However, we are told in Genesis 5:32 that Noah was 500 years old when he became the father of Shem, Ham and Japheth, and we are told in Genesis 7:6 that he was 600 years old when the floodwaters came. We are also told in Genesis 6:18 that when God spoke to Noah, and told him to build an ark, he told Noah that he would enter the ark with his sons and their wives. Therefore all three sons must have been of marriageable age, which reduces the time for building the ark to, at maximum, 80 years.

However, whether we believe in a worldwide flood, or a local one, 80 years would seem to provide more than enough time, not only to build the ark, but also for the whole inhabited world to find out *why* it was being built, and thus to know of their impending doom.

## The size of the ark

One reason for allowing a large amount of time for the building of the ark was the sheer size of it. Genesis 6:15 gives its dimensions as 450 feet long, 75 feet wide and 45 feet high. Arthur Custance stated:

> "With all the means later at their disposal, subsequent builders for four thousand years constructed seaworthy vessels that seldom seem to have exceeded 150 to 200 feet at the most. … It was not until 1884 apparently that a vessel, the Eturia, a Cunard liner, was built with a length exceeding that of the ark."

He therefore concluded that possibly people have mistaken the dimensions of the ark. However, Hugh Ross, also of the local flood persuasion, does not question the size of the ark, but rather expresses the view that, even at this enormous size, it would be unable to house the 10,000 species of living creatures that existed at that time. He, like Custance, therefore believes that only a *selection* of animals went aboard the ark with Noah and his family.

In contrast, Henry Morris who believes in a worldwide flood, feels that the simple fact that the ark was so large proves in itself that the flood was worldwide, as there would be no need for such an enormous construction if the flood was merely local. We therefore have a variety of conflicting opinions as to whether it was too large or too small. So again, we can see that the same facts can be interpreted totally differently, depending on our particular point of view.

## The stability of the ark

Some have questioned whether the ark would have been capable of withstanding the turbulence of the floodwaters for over a year, particularly in respect of a worldwide flood, but also in respect of an enormous local flood too. In answer to this particular criticism, Bernard Ramm gives some interesting details of the ark's size and stability in his book *The Christian View of Science and the Scripture*.

Whether we believe in a local or a worldwide flood, there is general agreement that the ark was an amazing structure, and well suited to its purpose of floating and surviving, rather than that of steering and manoeuvring.

> The ark had a door and three stories. The stories functioned the same as the staterooms in providing a division of animals and a bracing of the structure. The shape of the ark was boxy or angular, and not streamlined nor curved. With this shape it increased its carrying capacity by one third. It was a vessel designed for floating, not for sailing. A model was made by Peter Jansen of Holland, and Danish barges called *Fleuten* were modelled after the ark. These models proved that the ark had a greater capacity than curved or shaped vessels. They were very sea-worthy and almost impossible to capsize … The stability of such a barge is great and it increases as it sinks deeper into the water. The lower the centre of gravity the more difficult it is to capsize. If the centre of gravity were low enough the ark or barge could only be capsized if violently rolled over. Wherever the centre of gravity may have been in the ark, it certainly was a most stable vessel. (Bernard Ramm)

## 3) The reason the ark was filled with animals

Again, if we believe in a worldwide flood, the reason for filling the ark with animals is fairly straightforward. It was to save them from extinction. Genesis 6:17 says "I am going to bring floodwaters on the earth to destroy all life under the heavens, every creature that has the breath of life in it. Everything on earth will perish." In verse 19 God then adds:

> "You are to bring into the ark two of all living creatures, male and female, to keep them alive with you."

This seems fairly conclusive, and simple. The ark was built, not only to save Noah and his family, but also to save representative samples of all the kinds of animals living at that time.

## Problems with believing all the animals were on the ark

However, there are many arguments put forward against this scenario, mainly because there are quite a large number of difficulties in understanding *how* God did this. Firstly, as mentioned above, it is questioned whether the ark was big enough to house all the types of animals that existed at the time. Next, how did all the animals reach the ark? Arthur Custance summarises this problem by saying

> It is difficult to conceive how creatures accustomed to … very well-defined climatic conditions could pass through great stretches of country with entirely different environmental conditions as they made their way to the ark. Desert lizards from Central America, polar bears from the Arctic, kangaroos from Australia, and giraffes from Africa

would all have to make their way over thousands of miles of unfamiliar territory, and in one case by sea, to Asia Minor, where the environmental conditions might very well be 'unsuitable' for any of them. Multiply this circumstance to cover thousands of creatures who are so small that the journey could only be completed by about the tenth or even the twentieth generation descending from those who began it, and one gets a fair idea of the miraculous supervision required to assemble a crew sufficient to preserve every species from a global Flood.

Next, how did Noah and his family manage to look after so many animals for over a year? How did they cope with the larger, carnivorous animals, and keep them from becoming unmanageable, especially whilst weathering the turbulence of the floodwaters? How did they provide the right conditions for many animals that spend a lot of time in water, such as crocodiles and seals? How did they provide the right conditions for such diverse animals as polar bears and giraffes, the one requiring a cold climate, and the other requiring a hot climate? How did they store enough food and water for all of them to last a year, and how did they have access to all the different types of food necessary to feed all the diverse species? How did they dispose of all the waste products? And last but not least, how did these animals return to their natural habitats after the flood?

One commonly cited problem concerns Australian marsupials, which do not exist anywhere else in the world. Fossils in the rocks in Australia show that such animals have always existed in this area. Arthur Custance points out:

> The significance of this is that these creatures, if the Flood was world-wide, must have crossed the ocean and made a land journey covering thousands of miles to reach the ark

only to return later, reversing the sequence and finally swimming home in order to preserve the continuity between the fossils and the living forms peculiar to the area.

Because of all these difficulties, and many others, (e.g. how did plants and vegetation survive a worldwide flood, how did freshwater fish survive, etc.) it is easier to believe in a local flood, where it would not have been necessary to take samples of all animals from around the world on the ark. Consequently it would be unnecessary to answer any of these objections. Those who believe the flood was local, generally believe that the only animals on the ark with Noah were those which had become associated with man such as pets and domesticated animals. These, they argue, would have only existed where man existed, in the Mesopotamian valley, and so it was necessary to take them on the ark to prevent their extinction. However, it would not have been necessary to take any wild animals on the ark, as none of these would have been made extinct by a local flood. Their explanation as to why birds had to be taken on the ark is not quite so clear. It is suggested that perhaps some species were limited to this particular geographic area, and that these were also essential to man or the environment in some way, so that they could not be allowed to become extinct.

## Problems with believing only domestic animals were on the ark

However, as usual with this subject, in solving one set of difficulties, others are created. It is not just one verse in Genesis that refers to all the animals being saved. This is repeated many times by God, almost it seems, to emphasise that He does in fact mean all of them! These are listed below, but a quick read through Genesis 6 to 9 again will make it very difficult to think that God was only referring to domestic animals.

| Genesis 6:17 | I am going to bring floodwaters on the earth to destroy *all life* under the heavens, *every creature* that has the breath of life in it. *Everything* on earth will perish. |
|---|---|
| Genesis 7:2,3 | Take with you seven of *every kind of clean animal* … , and two of *every kind of unclean animal* …, and also seven of *every kind of bird*, … to keep their various kinds alive throughout the earth. |
| Genesis 7:4 | … I will wipe from the face of the earth *every living creature I have made.* |
| Genesis 7:14 | They had with them *every wild animal* according to its kind, *all livestock* according to their kinds, *every creature that moves along the ground* according to its kind and *every bird* according to its kind, *everything with wings.* |
| Genesis 7:15 | *Pairs of all creatures that have the breath of life in them* came to Noah and entered the ark. |
| Genesis 7:21 | *Every living thing that moved on the earth* perished – birds, livestock, wild animals, all the creatures that swarm over the earth, and all mankind. |
| Genesis 7:22 | *Everything on dry land that had the breath of life in its nostrils died.* |
| Genesis 7:23 | *Every living thing on the face of the earth* was wiped out; men and animals and the creatures that move along the ground and the birds of the air were wiped from the earth. Only Noah was left, and those with him in the ark. |
| Genesis 9:11 | … Never again will *all life* be cut off by the waters of a flood. |
| Genesis 9:15 | … Never again will the waters become a flood to destroy *all life.* |
| Genesis 9:17 | … This is the sign of the covenant I have established between me and *all life* on the earth. |

Although a number of these references could be explained by saying, again, that *all* has a limited meaning, there are many that cannot be explained. "All life under the heavens" would appear to refer to more than just domestic animals in Mesopotamia. "Every wild animal", "all livestock", "every creature that moves along the ground", "every bird" and "everything with wings" seems to cover all creatures, rather than just tame ones. And most importantly, Genesis 9:11 says:

> "I establish my covenant with you: Never again will all life be cut off by the waters of a flood; never again will there be a flood to destroy the earth."

If God was merely covenanting not to send a *local flood* again in which all the *local life* was destroyed, then this promise has been broken by Him many, many times over in the centuries since Noah's time, as there have been many local floods in many different places. This cannot be the case, as God can never break His word.

Therefore, if we concede that Genesis literally means all animal life on earth was destroyed, then we also have to concede that the flood must have been worldwide, as it cannot be argued that all animal life as well as all human life, was restricted to the Mesopotamian valley! We are therefore left with the set of problems listed above as to *how* God enabled all the animals to reach the ark, *how* He enabled Noah and his family to care for them all for well over a year in such a restricted environment, and *how* He enabled the surviving animals to return to the areas of the world they originally came from.

Henry Morris in *The Genesis Flood* makes an attempt to answer some of these questions, going into the numbers of animals, the size of the animals, how many species there were, and so on.

However, generally it seems that those who believe in a local flood tend to believe there were far more species alive in Noah's time, than those who believe in a worldwide flood. Those who believe in a local flood see the problem of fitting the whole lot into the ark as almost impossible. On the other hand, those that believe in a worldwide flood think there were fewer species, and demonstrate that the ark would have accommodated all the animals, with room for food storage as well.

There is a difference of opinion over whether, in Genesis 7:2, "seven of every kind of clean animal, a male and its mate" means seven pairs, or seven animals made up of three pairs and one extra. Henry Morris favours the lower number, suggesting that the extra animal was for the purposes of sacrifice once the flood was over, whereas Arthur Custance suggests that the larger number (fourteen) is the correct interpretation, which of course makes it all the more difficult to fit them all on the ark! The *NIV* translation of the Bible uses seven in the main text, but includes a footnote that it is possible that seven pairs is meant, so there is some legitimate doubt over exactly what is the original meaning.

To solve the problem of looking after all the animals for over a year, and all that would have entailed, it is suggested that large numbers of the animals would have gone into hibernation for an extended period. To solve the problem of the animals coming to and from the ark it is suggested that God used, or instilled, migration instincts in the animals. It is pointed out that both hibernation and migration instincts in animals are still not understood, and it is suggested as a possibility that these were instigated by God at the time of the flood.

Some believe that the world was still one land-mass at the time of the flood and that the 'canopy' of water would have created a uniformly temperate climate. If such were the case, then this would also solve the problem of the animals having to cross through seas and hostile territory.

These are interesting speculations, but there is of course nothing in the Bible to substantiate them. The Bible states facts about *what* happened, without going into explanations as to *how* God achieved them. In this sense the flood is similar to the creation passages, in that we are told about the fact of creation, but we are not told *how* God created.

## Conclusion

In conclusion on the subjects of the world population, the ark, and the animals, it can be seen that whichever view we favour there are problems and difficulties. The theory we prefer will tend to be coloured by which of these we feel to be more difficult to explain adequately.

# 5:
# During
# the flood
## (Genesis 7:11 – 8:14)

# 5: During the flood (Genesis 7:11 – 8:14)

These few verses describe the flood from start to finish; from the day Noah and his family entered the ark, to the day when the earth was completely dry again. The whole episode took just over one year, starting on the 17th day of the second month of Noah's 600th year (Genesis 7:11), and finishing on the 27th day of the second month of Noah's 601st year (Genesis 8:14).

One of the major differences between those who believe in a local flood and those who believe in a worldwide flood in approaching this passage is whether it is recorded from *Noah's* viewpoint, or from *God's* viewpoint. Those who believe in a local flood tend to think the whole narrative reads rather like a "ship's log", mentioning facts from Noah's point of view, and leaving out anything he would have had no first-hand knowledge of. It is for this reason, they explain, that the account reads *as if it is* universal, because from Noah's point of view, it was as good as being so. Bernard Ramm states:

> "the deluge was universal in so far as the area and observation and information of the narrator extended. Whatever existed beyond the scope of the narrator's knowledge the record is silent about."

Custance agrees with this scenario, and states:

> There are other indications from the text itself that the terms employed were the rather natural expression of a man overwhelmed by the devastation of his own community and

countryside. It is quite natural for a man in such circumstances to note that the water had risen above all the hills and mountains familiar to him from childhood. Knowing the draught of the ship and finding that the waters carried him over these familiar landmarks, he simply observed that the waters were at least fifteen cubits deep over their tops. The ark would not have drifted freely over them otherwise. It seems unlikely that this fact was supernaturally revealed to him, by the way the text reads (Gen. 7:19,20); yet he could not have known it by any other means if the reference is to the level of the water over the Alps or the Himalayas. But it would be quite clear to the captain of a ship, who had a pretty good idea of the draught of his vessel.

However, Henry Morris, of the worldwide flood persuasion has the following to say:

Actually, there is nothing in the entire passage to indicate that Noah is recording his personal impressions of the Flood. Instead, it is all seen from God's viewpoint. *God* looks down upon mankind and sees that it is corrupt; *God* chooses Noah and commands him to build the Ark; *God* calls him into the Ark and shuts the door; *God* remembers Noah and the animals and gradually brings the Flood to an end, and *God* commands them to leave the Ark and gives them His special covenant. In fact, Noah does not speak a single word in the entire passage, until the very end of the ninth chapter, when *God* puts into his mouth the remarkable prophecy concerning his three sons.

It is interesting to note that such conflicting views are held on this passage, and it may be helpful if we read it for ourselves, and come to our own conclusions.

*Noah's Flood: Local or Worldwide?*

## The authorship of the flood narrative

Another way to approach this question is to consider the authorship of the flood narrative. The authorship of the Pentateuch, including Genesis, is still the subject of debate among Bible scholars, but many believe that it was written by Moses. J. W. Wenham, in the introduction to the *New Bible Commentary Revised*, says:

> "we can regard Genesis-Numbers as the work of Moses … on the ground that Mosaic authorship best explains both its superlative qualities and its apparent deficiencies."

However, he adds:

> "we have no certain knowledge of their authorship, but the Pentateuch – and Genesis in particular – is unique."

Some believe that Moses, whilst not actually writing Genesis, compiled it from source documents that were first-hand accounts of what happened. We can then speculate that Noah took these documents with him into the ark, and added his own account to them.

If we go along with Mosaic authorship, then we have to believe that the whole account of the flood was related to Moses by divine inspiration, and that it is therefore written from God's point of view. If we believe that Moses compiled Genesis from inspired source documents, then it could be that the flood account was originally recorded by Noah. In this case, it *may* only include details from Noah's point of view, but equally it could also include details that only God could know of. He may have chosen to reveal to Noah additional details. For example, Genesis 7:22,23 states:

"Everything on dry land that had the breath of life in its nostrils died. Every living thing on the face of the earth was wiped out; men and animals and the creatures that move along the ground and the birds of the air were wiped from the earth. Only Noah was left, and those with him in the ark."

It seems unlikely that Noah would have known this for a fact, even if it did just relate to a local area. Without divine revelation, this would merely be a guess on Noah's part. Thus it is unlikely that the *entire* narrative could have been written from Noah's observation. Some of the information, by its very nature, had to be supplied by God. If this is the case, then it would be entirely possible for verse 19 (…and all the high mountains under the entire heavens were covered) to refer to the mountains worldwide, and not just to those which were within Noah's view.

Another reason for questioning the local flood theory relates to Noah's knowledge of the area surrounding where he had lived for 600 years. Some believe it is unlikely that he would have been so entirely ignorant of the topography of south-western Asia to have stated that all the mountains under the heavens were covered with water, when actually it only covered some of the lower ones nearby.

## Miracles

Another point that is often emphasised is that although God is quite ready and able to perform miracles whenever He wishes, we should not assume that He does so when alternative, natural explanations are available. This argument is often used by those who believe in a local flood, saying that to believe in a worldwide flood is only possible if we assume a large number of miracles took place, none of which are mentioned in the Bible. They are quick to affirm their belief in miracles *per se*, but see it as unacceptable to invoke unnecessary miracles. Custance states that we should not …

> "… *expect* to find miraculous elements where Scripture does not give reason to believe they were needed."

However, he does also say:

> "that one should not attempt to find a scientific explanation of every incident or factor in the Flood story".

This is sensible advice as the passage before us in this chapter includes several, clearly stated miracles. These include:

1) all the springs of the great deep burst forth (Genesis 7:11)
2) and the floodgates of the heavens were opened (Genesis 7:11)
3) rain fell on the earth for forty days and forty nights (Genesis 7:12)
4) pairs of all creatures … came to Noah and entered the ark (Genesis 7:15)
5) then the Lord shut him in (Genesis 7:16)

It is unclear exactly what phenomenon the first miracle refers to, and as we saw earlier in this booklet, various people have different ideas as to where all the water for the flood came from. On the face of it, though, it appears this must refer to water stored under the ground, and for this to 'burst forth' on the exact day that God told Noah and his family to enter the ark was a miracle.

The same is true of the 'floodgates of the heavens'. They were opened on the exact day that God told Noah and his family to enter the ark. It is not exactly clear what 'the floodgates of the heavens' were, although, as we have seen, Walt Brown, a Young-Earth creationist, agrees with secular scientists that it is unlikely that this refers to a canopy of water around the earth.

The next miracle was for rain to fall constantly for forty days and forty nights. Again, it is unclear how God could have caused rain to fall continuously for such an extended period of time.

The fourth miracle, as we have seen, involved migratory instincts in selected pairs of animals, perfect timing, and survival in environments hostile to some of the animals. They were also guided miraculously to the ark, and entered it of their own accord. The record does not say that Noah rounded them up, so even in the case of the local flood scenario, all the domestic animals made their way to the ark without any prompting from Noah. As we have also seen, there were possibly eighty years available for the building of the ark, and maybe some of this was necessary to allow enough time for the animals to migrate from distant lands.

The fifth miracle was that the Lord Himself shut them in the ark. Whether this involved some sort of final sealing of the door, in order that the whole structure was totally waterproof, we are not told. However, the Lord made sure they were all safely shut inside before the flood began.

Intrinsic to this passage are also a number of what we might term 'minor miracles'. Once Noah and his family were inside the ark, the ark and its contents were kept safe in the turbulent waters of the flood for an extended period of time. The animals must have remained manageable throughout an entire year, possibly due to hibernation, but possibly due to divine intervention keeping them relaxed and peaceful. Also, Noah and his family were given the ability to look after this enormous zoo, full of diverse animals, satisfactorily. Although none of this is mentioned in the passage, these 'minor miracles' must have taken place, whether the flood was local or worldwide, in order for the ark and its contents to survive successfully.

## The duration of the flood

As mentioned at the beginning of this chapter, the flood lasted just over one year. As the months were reckoned at 30 days long at that time, the entire period covered exactly 370 days – that is, one year and ten days from start to finish. This is a significant fact when considering whether the flood was worldwide or local. Some consider that it is more likely that a worldwide flood would last for such a length of time, rather than a local flood. In fact, no local flood has ever lasted for anywhere near that long. Even though the flood envisaged by Custance and others would have covered an enormous area of the Middle East, it is difficult to imagine why it would have taken such a long time to return to normal.

## The depth of the flood

In addition to the sheer length of time the flood lasted, the depth of the flood also has to be considered. Henry Morris considers this to be one of the most important Biblical arguments for a worldwide flood. Genesis 7:19,20 states:

> "They rose greatly on the earth, and all the high mountains under the entire heavens were covered. The waters rose and covered the mountains to a depth of more than twenty feet."

Most commentators agree that the reference to the 'depth of more than twenty feet (fifteen cubits)' relates to the draught of the ark, i.e. that the ark sank into the water to a depth of fifteen cubits when fully laden. If we look back at the dimensions of the ark in Genesis

6:15, the total height was 30 cubits, so that half would have been below the surface, and half above. When we appreciate this, we can understand why this particular detail was included. The ark floated freely on top of the water, and so it was clear that the mountains must have been covered by fifteen cubits of water, or more, as otherwise the ark would have grounded.

The problem with the local flood scenario is that if the mountains of Ararat were fully submerged to this level, then the land to the east and west of Mesopotamia must also have been submerged, and if this was the case then the flood, by necessity, must have continued on and covered most of the world, possibly with the exception of the Himalayas! Alternatively, a major additional geological miracle is necessary for a local flood: the land in the Middle East sunk, forming a saucer into which the floodwaters poured. However, it is the invoking of "unnecessary" miracles that the local flood theory seeks to avoid.

## Run off

Another argument put forward by Custance in favour of a local flood is the calculated rate of run-off rate of the floodwaters. Genesis 8:4 mentions that the ark came to rest on the mountains of Ararat on the seventeenth day of the seventh month, and that the tops of the mountains became visible on the first day of the tenth month (verse 5). Custance interprets this to mean that the ark settled at the very top of the highest mountain, and that after seventy-three days the water had gone down by just over twenty feet (being the draught of the ark) so that the top of the mountain it was resting on was just visible. Therefore by his calculation the water was running off at just over three inches a day – an impossibly slow rate for a worldwide flood, but an expected run-off rate for a local flood. (He quotes figures of a local flood where the run-off rate was about nine inches a day.)

In answer to this, Henry Morris suggests that the ark settled somewhere on the highest mountain, still well above all the other mountains. After seventy-three days the water had dropped sufficiently to reveal the tops of several of the surrounding mountains. Depending upon exactly what altitude the ark was grounded on Mount Ararat he calculated that the run-off rate would have been fifteen to twenty *feet* a day, thus suggesting a worldwide flood.

However, Dr. Victor Pearce states that Mount Ararat itself, at 17,000 feet high, is the highest peak, and that the surrounding peaks only reach 12,000 feet on average, a difference of 5,000 feet. It therefore seems that the run-off rate could have been as high as seventy feet a day if the ark was grounded at the summit of Mount Ararat. However, caution is needed here. Without knowing exactly how high up Mount Ararat the ark landed, it is impossible to say, with any real accuracy, what the actual run-off rate was. It therefore appears this is not a good argument for either side to use.

## The olive leaf

Another small point that is sometimes mentioned concerns the olive leaf plucked by the dove as evidence that dry land had appeared (Genesis 8:8-11). It can be calculated that the time that elapsed between the tops of the mountains first appearing, and the time of the olive leaf being plucked was 135 days, i.e. four and a half months. It has been questioned whether this is enough time for new growth to appear, but apparently olive trees are unusually hardy and can withstand severe damage, only to spring back to life when given the right conditions. It is suggested that this new growth probably appeared from broken branches that had taken root near the surface of the ground, as soon as the waters had receded. When Noah saw the olive leaf, Genesis 8:11 tells us that he knew the water had receded from the earth. Seven days later he sent the dove out again, and it never returned.

## The window in the ark

It was not until the first day of Noah's 601st year, when Noah removed the covering from the ark, that he "saw that the surface of the ground was dry" (Genesis 8:13). By calculation, this was twenty-nine days after he had sent the dove away for the final time. This is the first time a cover for the ark is mentioned, and whether this was the roof, or an additional structure, we are not told.

It is interesting that Noah did not know the ground was dry until he removed the cover from the ark. The window in the ark was apparently of no use in this respect. Therefore, although verse 5 tells us that the tops of the mountains became visible on the first day of the tenth month, it seems that this must have been a divinely revealed fact, recorded faithfully by Noah, but not observed by him at the time. Also, verse 5 *must* be understood to be referring only to the mountains near the ark, as obviously the tops of the Himalayas would have become visible to God long before the mountains of Ararat.

Verse 6 tells us that Noah opened a window he had made in the ark, and that it was through this that he sent the raven and the dove. This window was probably a solid panel of wood, as glass had not been invented. This would have been the only means of seeing out, and it did not give him a view of what was below the ark, which is why he needed the testimony of the birds.

In Genesis 6:16, the NIV refers to making a "roof" for the ark, whereas the KJV has "window". The Hebrew is *tsohar,* whose meaning in this context is fairly obscure, as it is translated *noon* on every other occasion in the Old Testament. It seems that whatever this opening was, it was very small in comparison to the size of the ark, possibly around 18 inches high (one cubit). Therefore, quite apart from not being able to see out, neither would much light have entered the ark until the covering was removed, almost one year after they had entered the ark. When it is appreciated just how dark and tomb-like the ark was, the possibility of the animals undergoing extended hibernation is seen to be all the more necessary, and the miracle of Noah and his family coping with everything even more amazing.

Finally, on the twenty-seventh day of the second month, the earth was completely dry, and it was time for Noah and his family to come out of the ark at last.

# 6:
# After
# the flood
## (Genesis 8:15-9:19)

# 6: After the flood (Genesis 8:15-9:19)

The first thing that Noah did after coming out of the ark was to build an altar and sacrifice some of the clean animals and birds to the Lord on it. This pleased the Lord, and He said in His heart:

> "Never again will I curse the ground because of man, even though every inclination of his heart is evil from childhood. And never again will I destroy all living creatures, as I have done." (Genesis 8:21)

In Genesis 3:17 God had cursed the ground because of Adam's sin, and through the flood, again the ground was cursed. But God decided at this point that enough was enough. Although the sinful nature of man is stated very clearly – his heart is evil *right from childhood* - God promised that He would never punish man's sinfulness by cursing the ground again.

## Changes after the flood

Having decided this "in his heart", God then spoke to Noah, and told him of a number of changes that were to take place, now that the flood was over. The details of these changes are given at the beginning of Genesis 9.

The first change is given in verse 2, and states that "the fear and dread of you will fall upon all the beasts of the earth and all the birds of the air … they are given into your hands." From this it appears that prior to the flood none of the animals, whether domestic or wild, were frightened or wary of humans, whether domestic or wild. This may partially explain how the task of looking after so many animals for so long, in a restricted space, for over a year was easier than if a similar experiment were to be carried out today. Because we live in a world where man's relationship with the animals is not like this, it may be difficult to understand that it was ever different in the past. However, we are told in Genesis 2:19 that God brought all the animals He had created to Adam for him to name them. There appeared to be no fear of man at that time. Also, in Isaiah 11:6-9, speaking of a time to come in the future, it is said:

> The wolf will live with the lamb, the leopard will lie down with the goat, the calf and the lion and the yearling together; and a little child will lead them. The cow will feed with the bear, their young will lie down together, and the lion will eat straw like the ox. The infant will play near the hole of the cobra, and the young child put his hand into the viper's nest. They will neither harm nor destroy on all my holy mountain, for the earth will be full of the knowledge of the Lord as the waters cover the sea.

It seems that God's original plan was for man to live in peace and harmony with the animals, but that man's sinfulness got in the way of God's original intentions.

The second change is mentioned in Genesis 9:3 which says,

> "Everything that lives and moves will be food for you. Just as I gave you the green plants, I now give you everything."

In Genesis 1:29 God had said,

"I give you every seed-bearing plant on the face of the whole earth and every tree that has fruit with seed in it. They will be yours for food."

Some expositors therefore conclude that before the flood man was vegetarian, and that only after the flood did humans start eating meat. However, it is clear that right from the early pages of Genesis animals were killed as sacrifices to God, long before the flood. Therefore some argue that man must have been meat-eating before the flood, as certainly from the time of Moses onwards sacrificed animals were eaten by the priests, levites, and also by the ordinary people. Also it has been pointed out by Bernard Ramm that kitchen middens (i.e. mounds of shells, animal bones and other such refuse) left behind at prehistoric settlements prove that man has been a meat-eater from antiquity. It may be that although God did not authorise meat-eating until after the flood, man, being wicked, had disobeyed Him in this.

The third change regards the taking of human life. Verse 5 says:

"And for your lifeblood I will surely demand an accounting … And from each man, too, I will demand an accounting for the life of his fellow man."

As mentioned at the beginning of chapter 4, before the flood murder and violence were commonplace among humans, so it seems that God immediately laid down guidelines after the flood for dealing with this very problem. It is not clear, however, exactly what the "accounting" referred to. Perhaps verse 6 gives a hint when it states "Whoever sheds the blood of man, by man shall his blood be shed", suggesting that a just system for dealing with murder should be set up, including the death penalty.

The fourth change stated is in verse 11, where God made a covenant that:

> "Never again will all life be cut off by the waters of a flood; never again will there be a flood to destroy the earth."

This promise seems to make more sense in the context of a worldwide flood, as there have been numerous local floods since Noah's day. However, in response to this we could argue that the flood of Noah's time, although not worldwide, was such an extensive flood that it far exceeded any others, and such that it destroyed all the lands of the ungodly people living in the ancient world (2 Peter 2:5).

The fifth change regards the rainbow. Verses 12 and 13 say:

> "This is the sign of the covenant I am making between me and you and every living creature with you, a covenant for all generations to come: I have set my rainbow in the clouds, and it will be the sign of the covenant between me and the earth."

Some suggest that this was a new phenomenon, unknown before the flood. They also suggest that there was no rain before the flood, as the two are obviously linked. Genesis 2:5,6 is usually quoted in this context:

> "... for the Lord God had not sent rain on the earth and there was no man to work the ground, but streams came up from the earth and watered the whole surface of the ground ..."

However, this refers to a time *before* Adam was created (mentioned in the next verse in Genesis 2:7), and did not necessarily continue for the next 1500 years or so until the flood. So the major change regarding the rainbow was that *it became a sign for mankind* of God's promise never to flood the whole earth again. The rainbow was not necessarily a new phenomenon, appearing for the first time because it had never rained before. Rather, God gave it a *new significance* after the flood, a **sign** that He would never flood the earth (or land) again.

## The spread of mankind

However, the first words that God said to Noah on his emergence from the ark are given in Genesis 9:1 which states:

> "Then God blessed Noah and his sons, saying to them, 'Be fruitful and increase in number and fill the earth.'"

The changes, the promises and the covenant, as described above, were specified afterwards. First and foremost, God wanted the earth to be repopulated with human beings. This was an exact reiteration of what He had said in Genesis 1:28:

> "God blessed them and said to them, 'Be fruitful and increase in number; fill the earth and subdue it.'"

Following this first command people had done just that, but they had also filled the earth with violence. This time God gave the same command, but added the death penalty to deal with any violence. He also promised never to destroy all people again with a flood, even though He knew they were *evil from childhood.*

Therefore, whether we believe there was a worldwide flood or not, unless we go along with the view that only *some* humans were wiped out by the flood, we have to accept that there must be, historically, two "cradles of civilisation", and not just one. The first flow of people came from Adam, and the Garden of Eden, and after 1,500 years "filled the earth". The second flow of people came from Noah and Mount Ararat, and spread throughout the earth over the ensuing years. The fact that mankind spread throughout the earth, starting with Noah and his family, is repeated a number of times in Genesis 9, 10 and 11. Genesis 9:19 says:

"These were the three sons of Noah, and from them came the people who were scattered over the earth."

Genesis 10:5 says:

"From these the maritime peoples spread out into their territories by their clans within their nations, each with its own language."

Genesis 10:32 says:

"These are the clans of Noah's sons, according to their lines of descent, within their nations. From these the nations spread out over the earth after the flood."

Genesis 11:9 says:

"That is why it was called Babel – because there the Lord confused the language of the whole world. From there the Lord scattered them over the face of the whole earth."

It is therefore clear that the Bible emphasises that mankind had a totally new beginning after the flood.

The question is, is there any non-Biblical evidence to support the view that there was a second cradle of civilisation, and that humanity spread out from one point again after the flood? There is some, as in chapter 2 we briefly mentioned evidence researched by Dr. Victor Pearce, regarding the apparent disappearance of all life on earth, during what is termed "the hiatus", a gap in culture and civilisation around 4000 to 5000 B.C. So, having spent the last three chapters looking at what the Bible has to say about the flood, we now return to consider what other, non-Biblical, evidence there is to support this event.

# 7:
# Anthropological evidence for the flood

# 7: Anthropological evidence for the flood

In chapter three, we looked at some of the geological implications of a worldwide flood, and also those for a large local flood. In chapters four, five and six we looked at the Biblical evidence for the flood. In this chapter we will look at the anthropological evidence for the flood – the science concerned with the study of human beings in the past. This evidence is mainly comprised of:

(1) the culture gap mentioned by Dr. Victor Pearce,
(2) information on the spread of mankind together with their racial groupings, and
(3) the many flood traditions which exist throughout the world.

## (1) The culture gap

Dr. Victor Pearce's main interests are in anthropology and archaeology, and he puts forward convincing evidence for the existence of Noah's flood by the study of the remains left behind by various different cultures in different parts of the world. As previously mentioned in chapter two, there is evidence of all life being wiped out in North America at about 5000 B.C. Then there was a long gap of 3000 years before life reappeared. This has been explained by some scientists to be the result of the volcanic eruption of Mount Masmara, but it has been suggested by Dr. Pearce that it is better explained by the flood.

In Europe there is a distinct culture gap between the copper-stone age, and the Bronze Age. Chalcolithic (i.e. copper Stone Age) pottery, and Ubaidian (i.e. Bronze Age) pottery, have been discovered by archaeologists at the same sites, one below the other. This pottery is entirely different and unconnected, and so some archaeologists have explained this by saying that the Ubaidians wiped out the Chalcolithic culture. However, as archaeology also confirms that there is a gap of about 1000 years between the copper-stone age and the Bronze Age, Dr. Pearce suggests that a better explanation would be Noah's flood, and that the Ubaidians in fact inhabited vacant land, rather than over-running the existing inhabitants. It has also mystified archaeologists why there was no progress in metallurgical techniques for 1000 years between the copper-stone age, and the Bronze Age, whereas the flood would provide a simple explanation.

In addition, it is pointed out that the culture gap is shorter in terms of time the closer it is to the plateau of Armenia and the Caucasus, i.e. the new point of dispersion of humanity. This gap widens as it follows a path westwards through Europe. This would be expected if there were a new beginning for humanity at this time, spreading out from one point.

Also mentioned briefly in chapter two were some of the changes that occurred in Egypt before and after the flood. Before the flood the people in Egypt used flint tools and copper-stone tools and lived on higher hills, because the valleys were wet marshlands. The whole area was lush and green. The people were farmers, and the area was full of animals. The inhabitants left rock drawings of the animals that can still be seen today. The whole area subsequently became a desert. 1000 years later a new migration of people from Mesopotamia, known as the Gerzians, entered the area. The hills were barren and dry, so they built low down on the mud flats of the Nile valley. The game animals had disappeared. Their tools and pottery were totally different, and belong to the early bronze-age culture. Archaeologists have considered this total change in culture as so fundamental that it cannot be explained by development only, and yet Noah's flood has never been put forward as a plausible explanation for this change.

## (2) The spread of mankind

This is a complicated subject, with many detailed arguments put forward to explain exactly where man came from originally. Arthur Custance summarises the basic problem well, as follows.

> Until the late nineteenth century, the Middle East had always been thought of as the Cradle of Civilisation. … If we limit ourselves to proto-history, i.e., that period which immediately preceded the sudden appearance of civilised man, almost every archaeological find has supported (this) more ancient view. Little by little the routes of migration of existing nations and tribes in the new World, in the Far East, in India, in Africa, in Scandinavia, in Russia, and in Europe have been reconstructed and the flow-lines consistently converge upon this area. Culturally speaking there is no other competitor as a Cradle of Civilisation.
>
> But the fossil remains of early man have been found almost everywhere except in this Cradle. This proved to be a source of embarrassment to pre-historians, because from an evolutionary point of view one would expect to find the first half-men multiplying in this area and leaving their fossil remains there. In the very nature of the case, more highly evolved hominids as they arose would move out, away from the central area.

Explanations have, of course, been offered to explain why this should be, and why there have been no traces of pre-historic man in the Central Highland of Asia, exactly where the start of civilisation has been traced back to.

Since the days of Charles Darwin, the fact that there may be no such thing as pre-historic man has never been considered a viable explanation. However, the plain archaeological evidence supports the Biblical narrative that man originated in the Iranian Highland plateau, and spread out from there. After the flood, there was a second start to mankind, originating with Noah from the mountains of Ararat. It is, in fact, far more difficult to support the conventional evolutionary understanding of the origins of man from the evidence available, which is understandable if the theory is incorrect!

Some have questioned whether the racial characteristics that have developed could possibly have done so in the time span available, on the assumption that Noah's flood took place around 6,000 to 7,000 years ago. One answer given to this is to use the example of the dog family. Most varieties of domestic dogs have been produced over the last 300 years, and the differences between the many varying breeds is enormous. In comparison, the variations in humans are minor. These may have arisen due to three main factors: natural selection, cultural preference and the isolation of small populations. The genetic variations for all the possibilities must however have been included in the original genetic material in Adam, created by God.

Natural selection occurs when certain parental genes in successive generations are filtered out, producing offspring with slightly different characteristics and less genetic variability. For example, fair-skinned people are more susceptible to certain health risks living near the equator, such as skin cancer, whereas dark-skinned people are more susceptible to developing rickets, as their skin screens out sunlight and tends to deprive them of vitamin D3, which in turn leads to rickets. Over many generations therefore light-skinned people would survive to reproductive age in the higher latitudes, whereas dark-skinned people would do so nearer the equator.

Cultural preference results from likes and dislikes. People who are similar in looks and characteristics are more likely to be attracted to each other, and conversely people often become prejudiced against those who are different from themselves. Over many generations this again leads to variety in the population.

Thirdly, the isolation of small populations can produce a different, and smaller, set of genetic characteristics than for an entire population, because the variety available in the gene pool of a small group of people is smaller than in a large group of people. Thus if a few members of a whole population move to an isolated region such as an island, subsequent generations will have different traits from the original population.

Dr. Victor Pearce includes a chart of the racial family tree computed from blood group gene frequencies compiled in 1963, based on information obtained from the Royal Anthropological Institute. The chart demonstrates one origin of all races and separates clearly three African groups from three European groups, with a third group being comprised of Asiatic, American Indian and Oceanic representatives. He suggests that the three main overall groupings may have resulted from Noah's three sons and their wives, which in its own small way supports the Biblical view of a second start to mankind after Noah's flood.

It is also interesting to consider the rate of population growth since the flood. Arthur Custance studied this question in detail, and by using certain population estimates, and calculating how often the human race doubled itself, worked backwards to discover roughly when it started. Not surprisingly, he came up with a date of about 4,500 years ago, which is the approximate date he favours for the flood! However, even if we question the accuracy of his calculations, it does tend to indicate that the human race cannot have started hundreds of thousands of years ago, or else it seems that the planet would have been over-run with human beings a long time ago.

As a particular illustration of the problems scientists have with sorting out the origins of mankind, and how they came to be distributed across the world in the way they are today, the Australian Aborigines are a prime example. Bill Bryson, in his book *Down Under,* has included some interesting comments on the puzzle they still present to anthropologists today.

> At some undetermined point in the great immensity of its past … (Australia) … was quietly invaded by a deeply inscrutable people, the Aborigines, who have no clearly evident racial or linguistic kinship to their neighbours in the region, and whose presence in Australia can be explained only by positing that they invented and mastered ocean-going craft at least 30,000 years in advance of anyone else in order to undertake an exodus, then forgot or abandoned nearly all that they had learned and scarcely ever bothered with the open sea again. It is an accomplishment so singular and extraordinary, so uncomfortable with scrutiny, that most histories breeze over it in a paragraph or two …

In other words, no one really knows how or when they got there, nor why they stayed there! We have the fact of their existence, and the rest is hypothesis. It has to be mentioned that the main problem is actually with the dating of some human bones found by a geologist in 1969 in New South Wales. They were dated at 23,000 years old. Before then it had been thought that the Aborigines had been in Australia for maybe 8,000 years, which in fact ties in much more neatly with the spread of mankind after Noah's flood. If the Aborigines were Noah's descendants, they would obviously

*Sorting out the origins of mankind*

have had no problem with building ocean-going vessels! In addition, we may expect some memory of a great flood in the form of traditions handed down from generation to generation. This is exactly what has been found, as there are a number of flood traditions found in various parts of Australia. This leads us to the third, and last, section of other evidence in favour of a large, catastrophic flood.

## (3) Flood traditions throughout the world

Collections of flood traditions have been made by a number of writers, and there are well over 100 such stories from all over the world. Arthur Custance wrote a paper entitled *Flood Traditions of the World* in which he included references to 140 such stories. There are apparently very few peoples without a flood tradition, and although Bernard Ramm cites Japan and Egypt as having none, Custance refers to there being one tradition in Egypt, and Dr. Victor Pearce refers to there being ancient Japanese records of the event.

We will briefly look at a general outline of these flood traditions. There are so many of them, all with a wealth of detail, that it will be necessary here to merely summarise the main common factors, and the main difference, between them.

The main common factors are the cause and effect of the flood, the fact that a favoured few escaped, and the method of their escape. In many traditions the cause of the flood is that the gods were angry with humans because of their wickedness, and wanted to destroy them. The result was that all but a few humans were destroyed as a punishment. These few usually escaped by building some sort of boat, or raft, thus escaping drowning in a flood. Often it is also added that animals were taken on board.

The main difference is that in each story the ark comes to rest on a mountain of local importance to the people who possess the tradition. The exception to this is the Biblical Hebrew account, where although they lived in Israel, the ark is recorded as coming to rest on Mount Ararat in Armenia, a land far away from their own immediate vicinity. This in itself tends to indicate that the account is more likely to be accurate.

## What do these flood traditions prove?

However, although the existence of these many traditions is not in dispute, it is what they actually prove that is. Henry Morris stated:

> "… anthropology has no right to decide one way or the `other concerning *the true significance of these flood legends*. All it can do is describe them and give some cautious guesses as to how they might be explained, such guesses being unavoidably coloured by the presuppositions of the one who makes them."

This is very true. Those that do believe in Noah's flood argue that, at the very least, they provide strong circumstantial evidence that such a flood did take place. However, those that deny that such a flood ever took place explain the existence of flood traditions in a variety of ways. Firstly, some fictitious traditions have been found among some groups of primitive peoples in widely separated areas, having several elements in common. So, some people conclude that the flood traditions are also fictitious. Although this could form a plausible explanation for them, so also would a real flood!

Next, some have considered at least part of these traditions have arisen because of small, local floods that had taken place in that particular area. This is a less viable explanation as it is unlikely that so many of the crucial details in the story would have been so similar if they were based on entirely different places and events. Custance states,

> Many natural disasters resulting from tidal waves have been reported in detail in the past, and one of the extraordinary things about them is that so many people, by one circumstance or another, survived the catastrophe. It is doubtful if there is any historical record of such an event completely obliterating a civilization so thoroughly that only one family survived. Yet virtually every one of these nearly 150 Flood stories record that this is exactly what did happen: only one party survived.

Some have suggested that missionaries were responsible for spreading the story of Noah's flood to primitive peoples. However, if this *were* the cause it is difficult to explain why there are differences in emphasis and detail in these traditions, and why there are no legends of other great Biblical miracles amongst such peoples (which undoubtedly missionaries would also have shared with them). Also, there are many remote tribes in the world who have such traditions, but who have never been visited by missionaries. It is also unlikely that missionaries would have concentrated all their efforts on relating the message of Noah's flood, rather than the gospel of salvation.

Although these traditions have been explained away with such arguments, it is probably true to say that if such traditions did not exist at all, this would have been used as a reasonable indication that such a flood never took place. In other words, to some people, although the lack of flood traditions would prove there was no flood, the existence of such traditions in abundance does not prove that there was!

## Worldwide or local?

However, if we do accept that such traditions reasonably indicate there was a flood, we then come to the question of whether they show in any way if it was worldwide, or just a large, local flood. Referring to this question Arthur Custance states:

> It is often claimed that the Flood Traditions, being worldwide, are proof of a universal flood. In point of fact they prove only that all races and tribes spring from Noah's family. In so far as these traditions relate to 'Noah's flood', and not to recollections of local floods, they could only signify that the family of Noah alone escaped and these scattered descendants carried family traditions with them. For if men all over the globe recorded the Great Flood in their area, then people all over the world survived to tell about it! But Scripture tells us that in fact only ONE family survived!

If some have claimed that the flood traditions prove there was a worldwide flood, Henry Morris is not one of these. Although he believes in a worldwide flood, he does not use the fact of these worldwide flood traditions to support this view. He merely states:

> "… conservative scholars do not look upon the flood traditions as constituting *proof* of the Noahic Deluge. Instead, they look upon these traditions as providing important *circumstantial evidence* for a flood that was at least anthropologically universal".

Thus he agrees with Custance on this point. The worldwide flood traditions may support a flood, but they do not support either view (local or universal) in preference to the other.

## Babylonian Flood Account

Lastly, this section on flood traditions would not be complete without mentioning the Babylonian flood account. This was briefly referred to in the introduction, where it was mentioned that those who believe Noah's flood never took place think the Biblical story was copied from the Babylonian flood traditions. In 1872 George Smith discovered the twelve tablets of the Gilgamesh Epic, the eleventh tablet of which describes a Babylonian flood. The original copies of the tablets date back to around 2000 B.C. The similarities and differences between the Biblical account and the Babylonian account have been summarised, and Bernard Ramm reproduced them as follows:

1) The Babylonian account is polytheistic and the Biblical account is monotheistic.
2) Both agree that the flood came as a divine punishment for man's sins.
3) The dimensions of the Babylonian ark are unreasonable (140x140x140 cubits), [i.e. 210x210x210 feet] whereas the proportions and size of the Biblical ark are about the same as those of modern ocean vessels.
4) The moral tone of the Babylonian epic is substandard. [i.e. immoral]
5) There is no mention of geological phenomena in the Babylonian account, *but the breaking up of the fountains of the deep means a rising ocean bed to bring waters in, and a falling one to drain them off.* [Ramm's own explanation is included in italics]
6) Both agree in the general details for the collecting of the animals, but the Babylonian account omits any reference to clean animals, and also includes other people in the ark. [i.e. more than eight]

7) In the Babylonian account the structure had a mast and a pilot.
8) The Babylonian flood lasted fourteen days and the Biblical flood one year and seventeen days.
9) The Babylonian account has a dove and a raven in reverse order and adds a swallow.
10) The Babylonian account has the altar after the flood but in a polytheistic context.
11) Both agree that the human race will not be destroyed after the flood.

Ramm comments on this, and believes that both came out of the *same* common ancient tradition and so both possess similarities. He says:

> The Babylonian account represents the tradition freely corrupted by human imagination; the Hebrew account is that which was kept chaste and pure through divine providence and then recorded through divine inspiration.

Christian scholars agree that the Babylonian flood account is one of the most remarkable confirmations of Genesis ever discovered in ancient literature.

However, liberal and secular scholars, instead of agreeing that the Babylonian account is a corrupted version of the Genesis account, have stated that, rather, the Genesis account is a corruption of the Gilgamesh Epic! Again, it seems to depend on the presuppositions of the person, which way the historical facts are interpreted. Thus both sides have spent some time in trying to prove their particular understanding.

Although there are many similarities between the two accounts, it is the differences that tend to prove (to Christians, at least!) that

Genesis in no way depends upon the Gilgamesh Epic as a source. Custance points out that the language of Genesis contains none of the polytheistic elements of the others, that it is sane and sober and matter-of-fact, and that little details such as a pilot and steering equipment are missing. He suggests that such facts indicate this was the first, and pure, account, as usually the details of second hand traditions are embellished, not simplified. It is also unlikely that a polytheistic account would have subsequently been transformed into a monotheistic account at a later date. The reverse is far more likely. Dr. Victor Pearce confirms that, in anthropology, monotheism is the more primitive conception, the supply of more and more intermediary gods or spirits between the High God and human beings being a later development. Pearce also quotes K. A. Kitchen in *The Bible in its World (1977)* who supports the opinion expressed by Custance mentioned above:

> The contrast between the monotheism and simplicity of the Hebrew account and the polytheism and elaboration of the Mesopotamian epic, is obvious to any reader. The common assumption that the Hebrew account is simply a purged and simplified version of the Babylonian legend (applied also to the Flood stories), is fallacious on methodological grounds. In the Ancient Near East, the rule is that simple accounts or traditions may give rise (by accretion and embellishment) to elaborate legends, but not vice versa. In the Ancient Orient, legends were not simplified or turned into pseudo history (historicized) as had been assumed for earlier Genesis records.

## Other flood tablets

Pearce also mentions that apart from the Babylonian flood tablets, archaeologists have also discovered other tablets produced by ancient peoples giving very full accounts of the flood. These include tablets from the Sumerians of south Mesopotamia and from a migrant Eblaite Society in Syria, both of which are far older than the Babylonian account. In addition there are also Hindu, Persian, Chinese, Japanese and Tibetan records of the same event. Andre Parrot, a French archaeologist, has stated that it is difficult to doubt that such detailed and persistent records have a factual basis and said, "the cataclysm was accompanied by destruction of such a scale and made such an impression that it became one of the themes of cuneiform literature."

Thus it seems that although the flood traditions throughout the world cannot be used to *prove* the existence of Noah's flood, they do give a strong indication that something of the sort must have happened thousands of years ago, despite the explanations for them given by those who prefer to believe that it could never have happened!

# Conclusion

# Conclusion

In this booklet we have looked at Noah's flood from three different angles – geological, theological and anthropological. What has probably become clear is that if we are Christians, and believe in the Bible as the inspired word of God, our interpretation of scientific facts and Biblical writings may differ from those who have no such belief. Facts are important, but our interpretation of those facts is also important, and can make an enormous difference to the conclusions we reach on any subject. As we have seen, differences also arise between Bible believing Christians as to how to understand Noah's flood – whether it was a large local flood, or whether it was a worldwide flood.

With respect to the geological evidence available for the flood, it seems that for any non-scientist, it is difficult to reach any definite conclusions. There are still many unsolved geological mysteries from the past, and maybe some day some of these will be solved. Until then, although I believe Noah's flood took place, I have to accept that that belief is mainly based upon the acceptance of the Bible as the inspired word of God. There are a number of geological facts which in my opinion adequately support this view, but which would not be sufficient to convince a sceptic. Having considered all the available information, to me it also seems more probable from the geological evidence that the flood was an extensive local flood, rather than a worldwide one.

With respect to the Biblical evidence, it is difficult to say whether Noah's flood was a large, local flood or a worldwide one, although again it seems more probable to me that what Genesis 6 to 8 describes is a very extensive, yet local flood. From Noah's point of view it may well have looked universal, but he would have had no means of proving this apart from divine revelation. As mentioned earlier, Psalm 104:5-9 seems to imply it was a local flood as these verses say God set a boundary for the waters that they *cannot cross*, and that *never again* will they cover the earth. This is in the context of the creation, when the earth originally …

"… was covered with the deep as with a garment …"

until…

"… they (the waters) flowed over the mountains, they went down into the valleys, to the place assigned for them." (See Genesis 1:2,9.)

If this understanding of these verses is correct, then this cannot have happened again in Noah's day. Those who accept the local flood theory also point to verses such as Job 38:8-11, and Proverbs 8:27-29 in support of this theory.

With respect to the anthropological evidence, although it supports a flood, it cannot be used to indicate whether it was local or worldwide. In either case, it is likely that the facts we have would actually be the same. However, in addition to the Biblical account itself, the strongest evidence for Noah's flood is in fact the anthropological evidence. When one considers the culture gap, which scientists admit exists, together with the study of the spread of mankind with three distinct racial groups, and then add the numerous flood traditions that exists, it is difficult to escape the conclusion that there must have been a very large flood in the distant past, as described in the Bible.

At the end of the day, it is our belief in what God tells us in His Word which is of paramount importance. However, He does not expect us to compromise our intelligence. We are never expected to exercise what is termed *blind faith*. He has given us enough factual evidence to support what is stated in Scripture, but whether we can be categorical as to whether the flood was local or worldwide is for each of us to decide.

# Appendix:
# The Canopy
# Theory

# Appendix: The Canopy Theory

Isaac Vail first proposed the "Canopy Theory" in 1874 in publications entitled *The Waters above the Firmament* and *The Deluge and its Cause*. He based his hypothesis on the mythology of the Greek, Roman, Egyptian and other ancient cultures, and used Genesis 1:6-8a to support his view:

> And God said, "Let there be an expanse between the waters to separate water from water." So God made the expanse and separated the water under the expanse from the water above it. And it was so. God called the expanse "sky".

Vail thought there was a vapour cylinder that surrounded the earth, which collapsed at the time of the flood, thus causing the worldwide flood. Since his time there have been a number of variations of this theme, involving a thin shell composed of water (either as a liquid, a gas or solid ice particles) surrounding the earth. This theory is invoked in answer to the question "Where did all the flood water come from?"

Whitcomb and Morris accepted this view in *The Genesis Flood* and cited three further verses in its support:

> Genesis 7:11b: … and the floodgates of the heavens were opened.

> Genesis 8:2: Now the springs of the deep and the floodgates of the heavens had been closed, and the rain had stopped falling from the sky.

2 Peter 3:5: But they deliberately forget that long ago by
God's word the heavens existed and the earth was
formed out of water and with water.

In my opinion, there are three questions that need to be answered
with respect to this theory:

1) Why was it originally proposed?
2) Is it scientifically tenable?
3) Is it supported by Scripture?

## 1) Why was the canopy theory originally proposed?

It was to answer the question "where did all the flood water come
from?" It was then unknown that large volumes of water were
stored in subterranean caverns below the surface of the earth. There
are now various theories as to how this subterranean water could
have produced a worldwide flood, thus meaning a canopy of water
above the earth is no longer required. One theory is that the earth
tilted on its axis, and the water was redistributed over the land
surface. Another is that the mid-oceanic rift ruptured around the
earth, and water gushed out of it into the air, and fell as rain.

## 2) Is it scientifically tenable?

It is not mentioned in secular scientific texts. It is only referred to
by scientific theologians who wish to explain where the flood water
came from. Some scientific theologians, however, have since set
out to disprove the theory from a scientific point of view, especially
since more plausible theories of where all the water came from
have been put forward. Their arguments against the possibility of a
canopy include such problems as light not penetrating a canopy,

atmospheric pressure being too high on the earth's surface, a solid ice canopy would be unstable and swiftly disintegrate, vapour or liquid would rapidly diffuse in the atmosphere, and so on. Therefore, from a purely scientific point of view, it seems there is little to substantiate it.

## 3) Is it supported by Scripture?

The four verses quoted above are those that are used to support the canopy theory. However, none of them clearly refers to a canopy of water above the earth, and I feel this idea has to be read into the verses quoted. Rather, it seems that the "water above the expanse" in Genesis 1:6 refers simply to clouds. This is how *the New Bible Commentary Revised* interprets verse 7: "The waters above are the clouds." There is no mention of a canopy of water.

However, Psalm 148 seems to confirm conclusively that Genesis 1:6 *cannot* refer to a canopy of water that collapsed at the flood. Psalm 148:1-6 says:

1) Praise the Lord. Praise the Lord from the heavens, praise him in the heights above.
2) Praise him, all his angels, praise him, all his heavenly hosts.
3) Praise him, sun and moon, praise him, all you shining stars.
4) Praise him, you highest heavens and *you waters above the skies*.
5) Let them praise the name of the Lord, for he commanded and they were created.
6) *He set them in place for ever and ever*; he gave a decree that will never pass away.

In verse 4, the psalmist praised "you waters above the skies." The same Hebrew words are used for "waters" and "skies" in this verse as in Genesis 1:6-8. The psalmist wrote this hundreds of years after the flood, and therefore cannot be referring to a canopy of water, which no longer existed. He must simply be referring to clouds in the sky. As the same words are used in Genesis, it seems logical to understand this as referring to clouds also.

Finally, Psalm 148:6 says that God "set them in place for ever and ever." If the "waters above the skies" were set in place *for ever and ever*, then they cannot have collapsed at the flood, and thus there is no scriptural support for the canopy theory.

# Bibliography

**Worldwide flood**

Dr E. K. Victor Pearce, *Evidence for Truth: Science* (Eagle:IPS, 1998)

John C. Whitcomb & Henry M. Morris, *The Genesis Flood* (Presbyterian and Reformed Publishing Co., 1961)

Walt Brown, *In the Beginning* (Center for Scientific Creation, 1995)


**Local flood**

Arthur Custance, *Flood Traditions of the World,* (Doorway Paper 18 - Doorway Publications 1957 –1972)

Arthur Custance, *The Flood: Local or Global?* (Doorway Paper 41 - Doorway Publications 1957 – 1972)

Dr Hugh Ross, *The Flood*, (series of 3 cassettes - Reasons to Believe, 1990)

Bernard Ramm, *The Christian View of Science and Scripture* (W. B. Eerdmans, 1954)


**Other**

Bill Bryson, *Down Under* (Doubleday, 2000)

If you have enjoyed this book by Sylvia Penny then you may also be interested in her book *Theories of Creation*. In this the author looks at five different ways of understanding Genesis 1, laying out succinctly and clearly the advantages and disadvantages of each view.

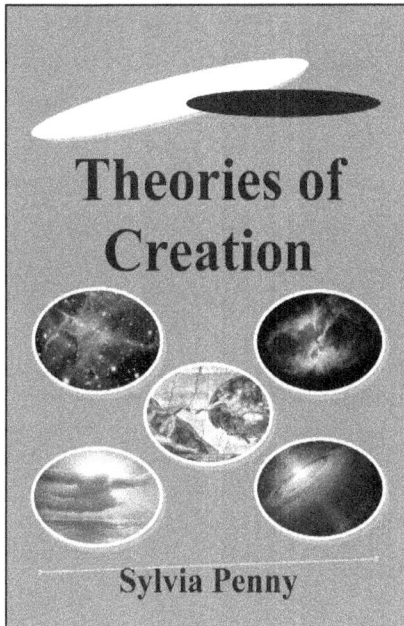

**Theories of Creation**

**Sylvia Penny**

# About the Author

Sylvia Penny was born in Bexleyheath, Kent, in 1956. She was educated at Basingstoke High School and Queen Mary's College, before studying accountancy at Oxford Polytechnic. She qualified as a Chartered Accountant and practised in the profession for a number of years, until she went to live in the USA with her husband and was a pastor's wife, taking an active role in the church. On returning to Britain she went back to the accountancy profession and now works part time as an accountant.

Other publications by Sylvia Penny include the books *Introducing God's Plan* (which she wrote with her husband Michael Penny) and *Salvation: Safe and Secure.* She also collated and edited *Woman to Woman,* a collection of articles for women by women and which has received a number of good reviews. An ideal book for women's ministry.

She has also written a number of study booklets including *The Seven Deadly Sins, Loving your Enemies, Lying, Forgiveness, Theories of Creation, Noah's Flood, Armianism or Calvinism?,* and *Resurrection: When?* (written with her husband Michael Penny).

Her latest major book is

**Details of all the above books, and other mentioned on these pages, can be seen on**

# www.obt.org.uk

**They can be ordered from that website and from**

**The Open Bible trust**
**Fordland Mount, Upper Basildon,**
**Reading, RG8 8LU, UK.**

**They are also available as eBooks from Amazon and Apple and as KDP paperbacks from Amazon.**

**Sylvia Penny is a regular contributor to**
*Search* **magazine which is published bi-monthly by The Open Bible Trust**

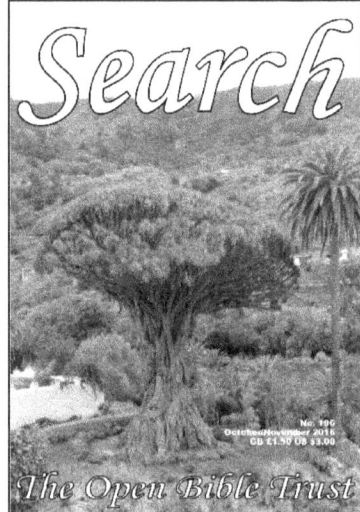

**For a free sample of**
**the Open Bible Trust's magazine *Search*,**
**please email**
**admin@obt.org.uk**

**or visit**
**www.obt.org.uk**

# Also by Sylvia Penny

## Satan through the Bible

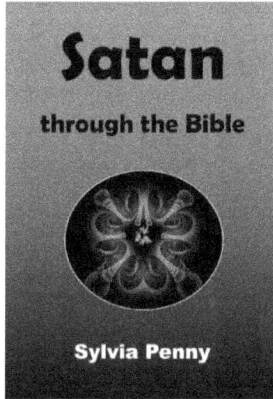

This is a comprehensive treatment of all that the Bible has to say about Satan. Starting with his creation before Eden, it follows him and his activities throughout the Bible, culminating with his demise in the lake of fire.

It considers many of his different names and titles, dealing with what they mean or signify. It discusses such issues as whether or not Satan is omnipresent, and just how much he knows and understands.

And we have details and explanations about every encounter Satan had with people including Eve and Job, Jesus and Judas, Peter and Paul, and many others.

We have a great and powerful enemy, and it is important that we have a Biblical view of who he is, what he is like, and how he can influence both individuals and society today.

Further details of the books on these pages,
can be seen on

# www.obt.org.uk

They can be ordered from that website and from

**The Open Bible trust**
**Fordland Mount, Upper Basildon,**
**Reading, RG8 8LU, UK.**

**They are also available as eBooks**
**from Amazon and Apple and as**
**KDP paperbacks from Amazon.**

# Woman to Woman
# By Sylvia Penny

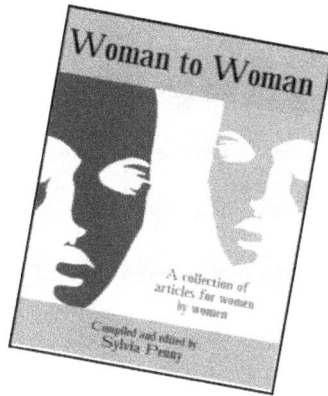

A collection of 60 articles by women for women compiled and edited by Sylvia Penny. Topics include:

- women in the Bible,
- Greek and Roman women,
- Paul and women,
- raising children,
- teenagers,
- marriage,
- swearing,
- abortion,
- and more.

"This book could be kept to hand for use in precious moments of quiet reflection as time allows – and enjoyed .... The book is nicely presented, about the right price for its size, and would make a very acceptable gift."
(Reviewed by Jan Macgregor in *Evangelicals Now*)

"It is both interesting and helpful .... I enjoyed the book. It is a good resource and easily dipped into."
(Reviewed by Rita Dollar in *Prophecy Today*.)

# Salvation

## Safe and Secure

### Sylvia Penny

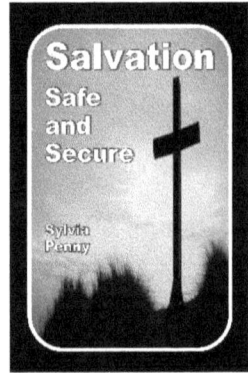

This important book is a thorough treatment of the subject of salvation, asking such questions as …

☐ What is it, exactly, that saves us?
☐ Is salvation secure?
☐ Can it be lost?
☐ What is 'conditional security'?

It deals with a wide number of issues such as …

- Salvation and works
- The doctrine of rewards
- Lordship salvation
- Free grace theology
- Assurance of salvation
- Why people lose their faith

# About this Book

## Noah's Flood:
## Local or Worldwide?

The great deluge is recorded in the early chapters of Genesis, but was it a universal flood or a local flood? Were all the mountains covered, or just those in that area? And what about the animals? Were these representatives of all animals from the *entire* world, or just those who were *local*? Or did the ark take only domestic animals?

There is evidence throughout the world of great flooding, but did it all take place at the same time? And what other evidence is there for a flood? Why have so many cultures a flood narrative as part of their ancient history?

In her usual thorough and fair manner, Sylvia Penny presents the evidence that supports, and questions, the main two views. All Christians will profit and learn from this book.

Publications of The Open Bible Trust must be in accordance with its evangelical, fundamental and dispensational basis. However, beyond this minimum, writers are free to express whatever beliefs they may have as their own understanding, provided that the aim in so doing is to further the object of The Open Bible Trust. A copy of the doctrinal basis is available on **www.obt.org.uk** or from:

**THE OPEN BIBLE TRUST**
**Fordland Mount, Upper Basildon,**
**Reading, RG8 8LU, UK**

www.ingramcontent.com/pod-product-compliance
Lightning Source LLC
Chambersburg PA
CBHW070528030426
42337CB00016B/2158